QUIET MOMENTS
with OSWALD CHAMBERS

QUIET MOMENTS
with OSWALD CHAMBERS

COMPILED BY

Heidi S. Hess

VB
VINE
BOOKS

SERVANT PUBLICATIONS
ANN ARBOR, MICHIGAN

© 1999 by Servant Publications
All rights reserved.

Vine Books is an imprint of Servant Publications especially designed to serve evangelical Christians.

Published by Servant Publications
P.O. Box 8617
Ann Arbor, Michigan 48107

Cover design: Left Coast Design, Portland, Oregon
Cover photograph: Courtesy of Discovery House Publishers

99 00 01 02 10 9 8 7 6 5 4 3 2 1

Printed in the United States of America
ISBN 1-56955-139-1

Library of Congress Cataloging-in-Publication Data

Chambers, Oswald, 1874-1917.
Quiet moments with Oswald Chambers / compiled by Heidi S. Hess.
   p. cm.
Includes bibliographical references.
ISBN 1-56955-139-1 (alk. paper)
1. Meditations.   I. Hess, Heidi.   II. Title.
BV4832.2.C513   1999
242—dc21   98-52844
                                                                      CIP

Dedication

For Craig, who reminds me every day of the magnificent gifts
God has in store for those who love Him
and for our parents, who made the giving possible.

Introduction

As a teenager I was laid up for months after a bad car accident. I spent the time reading and cross-stitching little reminders of God's loving faithfulness toward me. This sampler, my favorite, graces my office wall—a simple yet eloquent reminder of more difficult days gone by.

If you are going to be used by God,
He will take you through a multitude of experiences
That were not meant for you at all.
They are meant to make you useful in His hands.
OSWALD CHAMBERS

I later discovered that Oswald Chambers (1874-1917) was a man who knew what it meant to live a vital Christian life, devoid of religious platitudes and full of holy fire. This zealous Scotsman served God as an itinerant evangelist and teacher, and brandished the Word of God like a well-honed sword. He died "with his boots on" at the age of forty-three—of complications from a ruptured appendix—while serving as a YMCA chaplain to British troops in Egypt during World War I. His widow, Biddy, compiled most of Chambers' many books from his sermons, preached over the course of their seven-year marriage.

Though Chambers is best remembered for the classic *My Utmost for His Highest*, these selections have been taken from a number of his lesser-known works, which are listed at the back of this book. So make yourself comfortable and spend a few quiet moments with a man whose short life was spent in unswerving devotion and blind obedience to the cause of Christ.

1
Many Gates to the Soul

There are many ways in which a man's life may be suddenly struck by an immortal moment, when the true issues of his life, "the spirit's true endowments, stand out plainly from its false ones," and he knows in that moment whether he is "pursuing the right way or the wrong way, to its triumph or undoing." Such a moment may come by conviction of sin, or it may come through the opening up of the vast isolation of a man's own nature which makes him afraid. Or it may come with the feeling that somewhere he will meet One who will put him on the way to solve his implicit questions, One who will satisfy the last aching abyss of the human heart, and put within his hands the key to unlock the secret treasures of life. There are many gates into the holy city, and many avenues by which God may enter the human soul.

2
The Way of Gladness

One of the significant things about those who are in the way [of discipleship] is that they have a strong family likeness to Jesus; His peace marks them in an altogether conspicuous manner. The light of morning is on their faces, and the joy of the endless life is in their hearts. Wherever they go, men are gladdened or healed, or made conscious of a need.

The way to the fulfillment of all life's highest ideals and its deepest longings is the Lord Jesus Christ Himself. How patiently He waits until, having battered ourselves against the impregnable bars of our universe, we turn at last, humbled and bruised, to His arms, and find that all our fightings and fears, all our willfulness and waywardness, were unnecessary had we but been simple enough to come to Him at the first.

3
Spiritual Matchmaking

"He must increase, but I must decrease" (Jn 3:30).

The most delicate mission on earth is to win souls for Jesus without deranging their affections and affinities and sympathies by our own personal fascination. There is neither discouragement nor pensive humility in John's statement, but the passionate realization of his position. As Christian workers we are about the most sacred business, seeking to win souls to the Lord Jesus, ministering to the holy relationship of bridegroom and bride. That is our business, and we must be watchful lest any mood or disposition of our own should give a false impression of the Bridegroom and scare away the prospective bride. We are here for His sake, and we have to take care lest we damage His reputation. It may sometimes mean scaring a soul away from ourselves in order that Jesus Christ's attraction may tell.

4
God's Mysterious Plan

"But rejoice to the extent that you partake of Christ's sufferings" (1 Pt 4:13).

If we are going to be used by God, He will take us through a multitude of experiences that are not meant for us at all, but meant to make us useful in His hands. There are things we go through which are unexplainable on any other line, and the nearer we get to God the more inexplicable the way seems. It is only on looking back and by getting an explanation from God's Word that we understand His dealings with us. It is part of Christian culture to know what God is after. Jesus Christ suffered "according to the will of God"; He did not suffer in the way we suffer as individuals. In the person of Jesus Christ we have the universal presentation of the whole of the human race.

5
The Confident Saint

The stars do their work without fuss; God does His work without fuss, and saints do their work without fuss. The people who are always desperately active are a nuisance; it is through the saints who are one with Him that God is doing things all the time. The broken and the jaded and the twisted are being ministered to by God through the saints who are not overcome by their own panic, who because of their oneness with Him are absolutely at rest, consequently He can work through them. A sanctified saint remains perfectly confident in God, because sanctification is not something the Lord gives me, sanctification is *Himself in me.* There is only one holiness, the holiness of God, and only one sanctification, the sanctification that has its origin in Jesus Christ. "But of Him you are in Christ Jesus, who became for us … sanctification" (1 Cor 1:30). A sanctified saint is at leisure from himself and his own affairs, confident that God is bringing all things out well.

6
Tested at the Point of Strength

You have borne the burden and heat of the day, been through the big test, now beware of the undertime, the afterpart of the day spiritually. We are apt to forget that there is always an afterward, and that it comes close on the heels of the present. It is in the aftermath of a great spiritual transaction that the "retired sphere of the leasts" begins to sap. "Now that I have been through the supreme crisis, it is not in the least likely that I shall turn to the things of the world." It is the least likely thing that is the peril. The Bible characters never fell on their weak points but on their strong ones; unguarded strength is double weakness. It is in the afterpart of the day spiritually that we have to be alert.

7
Strive to Enter Through the Narrow Gate

If you make a moral struggle and gain a moral victory, you will be a benefit to all you come across, whereas if you do not struggle, you act as a moral pollution. Gain a moral victory in chastity or in your emotional life, it may be known to no one but yourself, and you are an untold benefit to everyone else; but if you refuse to struggle, everyone else is weakened. This is a recognized psychological law, although little known. Struggle to gain the mastery over selfishness, and you will be a tremendous assistance; but if you don't overcome the tendency to spiritual sluggishness and self-indulgence, you are a hindrance to all around you. These things are intangible, but they are there, and Jesus says to us, "Strive to enter through the narrow gate." You never get through alone. If you struggle to get through, others are the stronger and better for knowing you.

8
Wait Silently for God

Is silent prayer to us an experience of waiting upon God, or is it a "cotton wool" experience? Utterly dim and dark? A time which we simply endure until it is over? If you want discerning vision about anything, you have to make an effort and call in your wandering attention. Mental woolgathering can be stopped if the will is roused. Prayer is an effort of will, and the great battle in prayer is the overcoming of mental woolgathering. We put things down to the devil when we should put them down to our own inability to concentrate. "My soul, wait silently for God alone," that is, "pull yourself together and be silent before God."

"MY SOUL, wait silently for God alone."

Stop all false hurry and spend time in communion with God. Think of the benediction which comes to your disposition by waiting upon God! Some of us are in such a hurry that we distort God's blessings for ourselves and for others. "Wait silently on God alone"; to do that will demand at the beginning the severest mental effort we have ever put forth.

9
Love and Obedience

Natural individuality holds strongly to natural relationships. The natural relationships on which individuality is based are these: father, mother, brothers and sisters, husband and wife, children, self-interest. These are the relationships with which our Lord says we are likely to clash if we are going to be His disciples. If the clash comes, He says it must be instant obedience to Him (see Lk 14:26). Our obedience to Jesus Christ is going to cost other people a great deal. And if we refuse to go on because of the cost to them or because of the stab and the jeer, we may find that we have prevented the call of God coming to other lives; whereas if we will go through with God, all these natural relationships will be given to our credit spiritually at the last.

10
Who Is Christ to Me?

"And Simon Peter answered and said, 'You are the Christ, the Son of the living God.' Jesus answered and said to him, 'Blessed are you, Simon Bar-Jona, for flesh and blood has not revealed this to you, but My Father who is in heaven'" (Mt 16:16-17).

The Lord Jesus Christ is not a commonsensical fact; that is, we do not understand Him by means of our common sense. The disciples at this stage only knew Jesus Christ by means of their common sense—by their eyes and ears and all the powers of common sense men—they had never discerned who He was. Our Lord is a revelation fact, and when Peter confessed, "You are the Christ, the Son of the living God," Jesus Christ recognized from whom he had received the revelation—not from his common sense, but from God. Is Jesus Christ a revelation to me, or is He simply a historical character?

11
Misplaced Devotion

If Jesus Christ is not revealed to us, it is because we have views of our own, and we want to bend everything to those views. To realize Christ we must come to Him. That is, we must learn to trust someone other than ourselves, and to do this, we must deliberately efface ourselves.

Devotion and piety are apt to be the greatest opponents of Jesus Christ, because we devote ourselves to devotion instead of to Him. To surrender to God is not to surrender to the fact that we have surrendered. That is not coming at all. To come means that we come to God in complete abandonment and give ourselves right over to Him and leave ourselves in His hands. The Lord Jesus Christ is the one person to whom we ought to yield, and we must be perfectly certain that it is to Himself that we are yielding. Do not be sorry if other appeals find you stiff-necked and unyielding; but be sorry if, when He says, "Come to Me," you do not come. The attitude of coming is that the will resolutely lets go of everything and deliberately commits all to Him.

12

A Deadly Compromise

The first sign of the dethroning of Jesus is the apparent absence of the devil, and the peaceful propaganda that is spread after he has withdrawn. Will the church that bows down and compromises succeed? Of course it will, it is the very thing that the natural man wants. This line of temptation as revealed by our Lord is the most appallingly subtle of all.

Temptation yielded to is lust deified. In the Bible, the term "lust" is used of other things than merely of immorality. It is the spirit of "I must have it at once; I will have my desire gratified, and I will tolerate no restraint." Each temptation of our Lord contains the deification of lust: "You will get the kingship of the world at once by putting men's needs first. Use signs and wonders, compromise with evil, judiciously harmonize with natural forces, and you will get the kingship of men at once." At the heart of every one of our Lord's answers are these words: "For I have come down from heaven, not to do My own will, but the will of Him who sent Me"(Jn 6:38).

13
Active Christianity

We have the notion at first that when we are saved and sanctified by God's supernatural grace, He does not require us to do anything, but it is only then that He begins to require anything of us. God did not shield His own Son; not only did He not shield Him, but He allowed Him to be driven into the wilderness to be tempted of the devil. After the baptism of Jesus and the descent of the Holy Spirit upon Him, God took His sheltering hand off Him, as it were, and let the devil do his worst. So after the work of sanctification, when the life of a saint really begins, God lifts His hand off and lets the world, the flesh, and the devil do their worst, for He is assured that "greater is He who is in you, than he who is in the world."

14
Born Not for Mountains but Valleys

Never mistake the wonderful visions God gives you for reality, but watch, for after the vision you will be brought straight down into the valley. We are not made for the mountains; we are made for the valley. Thank God for the mountains, for the glorious spiritual realization of who Jesus Christ is; but can we face things as they actually are in the light of the reality of Jesus Christ? Or do things as they are efface altogether our faith in Him and drive us into a panic? When Jesus said, "I go to prepare a place for you," it was to the cross He went. Through His cross He prepared a place for us to "sit with him in the heavenly places, in Christ Jesus," now not by and by. When we get to the cross, we do not go through and out the other side. We abide in the life to which the cross is the gateway; and the characteristic of the life is deep and profound sacrifice to God. We know who our Lord is by the power of his Spirit; we are strongly confident in Him, and the reality of our relationship to Him works out all the time in the actualities of our ordinary life.

15

True Self-Denial

Always notice the "if" in connection with discipleship, there is never any compulsion. "If anyone comes to me, and does not hate… he cannot be my disciple." He may be anything else—a very fascinating person, a most delightful asset to modern civilization—but Jesus Christ says, "he cannot be my disciple." A man may be saved without being a disciple, and it is the point of discipleship that is always kicked against. Our Lord is not talking of eternal salvation but of the possibility of our being of temporal worth to Himself. How many of us are of any worth to Jesus Christ?

16
God Uses Us at Our Point of Weakness

Be absolutely abandoned to God, it is only your own reputation that is at stake. People will not discredit God; they will only think you are a fool.

After the resurrection, Jesus Christ did not invite the disciples to a time of communion on the Mount of Transfiguration, He said—"Feed My sheep." When God gives a person work to do, it is seldom work that seems at all appropriate to his natural ability. Paul, lion-hearted genius though he was, spent his time teaching the most ignorant people. The evidence that we are in love with God is that we identify ourselves with His interests in others, and other people are the exact expression of what we ourselves are. That is the humiliating thing! Jesus Christ came down to a most miserably insignificant people to redeem them. When He has lifted us into relationship with Himself, He expects us to identify ourselves with His interests in others.

17
The Pursuit of Peace

"My peace I give to you" (Jn 14:27). The idea of peace in connection with personality is that every power is in perfect working order to the limit of activity. That is what Jesus means when He says "My peace." Never connect the idea of stagnation or being jaded with peace. Health is physical peace, but it is not stagnation; health is the perfection of physical activity. Virtue is moral peace, but it is not innocence; virtue is the perfection of moral activity. Holiness is spiritual peace, but it is not quietness; holiness is the most intense spiritual activity.

It is easy to conceive of a personality full of joy and peace, but isolated. The striking thing about our Lord is that He was never isolated. "If anyone loves Me," He said, "We will come to him, and make our home with him." The conception is that of perfect converse and union; the abiding of the Trinity with the saint. The destiny of mankind in the purpose of God is not to do something, but to be something; "that they may be one even as We are."

18
Abiding Under the Shadow

What kind of Lord Jesus do we have? Is He the all-powerful God in our present circumstances, in our providential setting? Is He the all-wise God of our thinking and our planning? Is He the ever-present God, "closer than breathing, nearer than hands or feet"? If He is, we know what it means to "abide under the shadow of the Almighty." No one can tell us where the shadow of the Almighty is; we have to find it out for ourselves.

When by obedience we have discovered where it is, we must abide there—"No evil shall befall you, nor shall any plague come near your dwelling." That is the life that is more than conqueror because the joy of the Lord has become its strength; and that soul is on the way to entering ultimately into the joy of the Lord.

19
The Death of Disobedience

There is quite sufficient evidence to indicate that when Adam's spirit, soul, and body were united in perfect faith and love to God, his soul was the medium through which the marvelous life of the Spirit of God was brought down. The very image of God was brought down into his material body and it was clothed in an inconceivable splendor of light until the whole person was in the likeness of God.

The moment he disobeyed, the connection with God was shut off, and spirit, soul, and body tumbled into death that instant. The fact of dissolving into dust in a few years' time is nothing more than death visible. Do not bring the idea of time in at all. Death happened instantly in spirit, soul, and body, spiritually and psychically. The connecting link with deity was gone, and the human spirit, soul, and body tumbled into disintegrating death; and when they "heard the sound of the Lord God walking in the garden" (Gn 3:8), they were terrified and hid themselves.

20
Holiness: Morality on Fire

Jesus Christ is going to change "our lowly body" and conform it "to His glorious body" (Phil 3:21), and the result will be not an intuitive innocence only, but a conscious manly and womanly holiness. *Holiness* is the expression of the new disposition God has given us maintained against all odds. Holiness is militant, Satan is continually pressing and ardent, but holiness maintains itself. It is morality on fire and transfigured into the likeness of God. Holiness is not only what God gives me, but what I manifest that God has given me.

I manifest this brilliant holiness by my reaction against sin, the world, and the devil. Wherever God's saints are in the world they are protected by a wall of fire which they do not see, but Satan does. "The wicked one does not touch him" (1 Jn 5:18).

21
Life in the Spirit

As soon as the Holy Spirit comes in as life and as light, He will chase through every avenue of our minds; His light will penetrate every recess of our hearts; He will chase His light through every affection of our souls, and make us know what sin is. The Holy Spirit convicts of sin, humanity does not. The Holy Spirit is that marvelous Spirit that kept our Lord when He was incarnate—spirit, soul, and body—in perfect harmony with absolute Deity.

When Jesus said, "You have no life in you," He meant the life He lived; and we cannot have that life saving through Him. He who believes on the Son has everlasting life (see Jn 3:16)—the life Jesus lived, Holy Spirit life. The Holy Spirit will take us, spirit, soul, and body, and bring us back into communion with God; and if we obey the light He gives, He will lead us into identification with the death of Jesus until we know experientially that our old man, my right to myself, is crucified with Him and our human nature is free now to obey the commands of God.

22
Changed With God's Glory

God is not after satisfying us and glorifying us; He wants to manifest in us what His Son can do. "When He comes ... to be glorified in His saints and to be admired among all those who believe" (2 Thes 1:10). The invasion of the life of Jesus Christ makes us sons and daughters of God. These are things that the angels desire to look into. It is as if they look down on us and say, "Look at that woman, how wonderfully like Jesus Christ she is; she used not to be, but look at her now. We know Jesus Christ did it, but we wonder how?" Or, "Look at that man, he is just like his Master, how did Jesus Christ do it?" Thank God we are not going to be angels, we are going to be something tenfold better. By the redemption of Jesus Christ there is a time coming when our bodies will be in the image of God. "Our lowly body" is to be conformed to "His glorious body" (Phil 3:21) and our bodies will bear the image of God as our spirits do.

23

What Happens to the Soul at Death?

The spirit in the human being which holds his soul and body together is entirely different from the spirit of an animal; it is the human spirit which God created when He breathed into Adam's nostrils the breath of life. God did not make the man a little god; He breathed into his nostrils the spirit which became humanity's distinct spirit, "and man became a living soul."

Where does someone's spirit go when he dies? "Who knows the spirit of the sons of men, which goes upward, and the spirit of the animal, which goes down to the earth?" (Eccl 3:21). Scientists tell us that death is a molecular disturbance, that when we die we are distributed into the spirit of entire nature. The Bible says that the spirit of a man goes back to God. This does not imply that a person's spirit is absorbed into God; but that the human spirit goes back to God with the characteristics on it for either judgment or praise.

24
Using the Power of the Soul for Good

Knowledge of evil broadens a person's mind, makes him tolerant, but paralyzes his action. Knowledge of good broadens a person's mind, makes him intolerant of all sin, and shows itself in intense activity. A bad person, an evil-minded individual, is amazingly tolerant of everything and everyone, no matter whether they are good or bad, Christian or not, but his power of action is paralyzed entirely. He is tolerant of everything—the devil, the flesh, the world, sin, and everything else.

Jesus Christ never tolerated sin for one moment, and when His nature is getting its way in a soul the same intolerance is shown, and it manifests itself "not with eye service" (Eph 6:6). If I am a servant I won't serve my master or mistress with this power of my soul realizing I have power to deceive. I will use it to show that I belong to Jesus Christ. Neither shall I use this power of my soul to do what I like with my body. "Not with eye service, as menpleasers, but as bondservants of Christ, doing the will of God from the heart" (Eph 6:6).

25
The Power of Freedom

Whenever Jesus Christ presents the gospel of God to a soul, it is always on the line of "Are you willing?" There is never any coercion. God has so constituted us that there must be a free willingness on our part.

This power is at once the most fearful and the most glorious power. A human soul can withstand the devil successfully, and it can also withstand God successfully. This self-living power is the essence of the human spirit, which is as immortal as God's Spirit and as indestructible; whether the human spirit be good or bad, it is as immortal as God. This power of the soul enables it to put itself on a par with God; this is the very essence of Satan. The power that can make someone either a peer of the Lord or a peer of the devil is the most terrible power of the soul. Jesus Christ is referring to this power when He says, "I lay down my life of Myself; no man takes it from me" (Jn 10:17-18).

26
Practicing Goodness

If you obey the Spirit of God and practice in your physical life all that God has put in your heart by His Spirit, when the crisis comes you will find your nature will stand by you. So many people misunderstand why they fall. It comes from this idea, "Now I have received the grace of God, I am all right." Paul says he did not "frustrate the grace of God," that is, receive it in vain. If we do not go on practicing day by day and week by week, working out what God has worked in, when a crisis comes God's grace is there right enough, but our natures are not. Our natures have not been brought into line by practice and consequently do not stand by us, and down we go and then we blame God. We must bring our bodily lives into line by practice day by day, hour by hour, moment by moment, then when the crisis comes we shall find not only God's grace but our own natures will stand by us, and the crisis will pass without any disaster at all. Exactly the opposite will happen—the soul will be built up into a stronger attitude toward God.

27
Cherishing the Supernatural

"Lord, do You want us to command fire to come down from heaven and consume them?" (Lk 9:54). The disciples knew Jesus Christ well enough to know that He had intimacy with supernatural powers, but they had yet to learn that it is possible to scathe sin and at the same time serve one's self. "But He turned and rebuked them, and said, 'You do not know what manner of spirit you are of'" (Lk 9:55). It is possible to do right in the wrong spirit. These were the very people who a little while afterward asked that they might sit, "one on Your right hand, and the other on Your left, in Your glory"; and one of them (see Acts 8) was sent down by God to Samaria, where he realized what the fire was that God was to send, that is, the fire of the Holy Spirit.

"For we do not wrestle against flesh and blood, but against principalities, against powers" (Eph 6:12). This has to do not with the bodily side of things, but with the supernatural. We are surrounded immediately by powers and forces which we cannot discern physically. "I do not want you to have fellowship with demons. You cannot drink the cup of the Lord and the cup of demons" (1 Cor 10:20-21). You can always tell whether Christians are spiritually minded by their attitude to the supernatural.

28
Prayer and Meditation

A great many delightful people mistake meditation for prayer; meditation often accompanies prayer, but it is not prayer. It is simply the power of the natural heart to get to the middle of things. Prayer is asking, whereby God puts processes to work and creates things which are not in existence until we ask. It is not that God withholds, but He has so constituted things on the ground of redemption that they cannot be given until we ask. Prayer is definite talk to God, around which God puts an atmosphere, and we get answers back. Meditation has a reflex action; people without an ounce of the Spirit of God in them can meditate, but that is not prayer. This fundamental distinction is frequently obscured.

29
Questions of the Heart

"For the word of God ... is a discerner of the thoughts and intents of the heart" (Heb 4:12; see also Gn 8:21; 17:17; 24:45; Eccl 1:16; Mt 24:48).

According to the Bible, thinking exists in the heart, and that is the region with which the Spirit of God deals. We may take it as a general rule that Jesus Christ never answers any questions that spring from a person's head, because the questions which spring from our brains are always borrowed from some book we have read, or from someone we have heard speak; but the questions that spring from our hearts, the real problems that vex us, Jesus Christ answers those. The questions He came to deal with are those that spring from the implicit center. These problems may be difficult to state in words, but they are the problems Jesus Christ will solve.

30

Human Goodness or True Virtue?

There is a difference between the modern way of looking at people and the way the Bible looks at them. The modern way of looking at people and their virtues is to say, "What a wonderful promise of what humanity is going to be; given right conditions, we will develop and be all right." The Bible looks at a person and says, "He must be born again; he is a ruin, and only the Spirit of God can remake him." We cannot patch up our natural virtues and make them come up to Jesus Christ's standard. No natural love, no natural patience, no natural purity, no natural forgiveness can come anywhere near what Jesus Christ demands. The hymn has it rightly:

> And every virtue we possess,
> And every victory won,
> And every thought of holiness,
> Are His alone.

31
Spiritual Prejudice

Until the Holy Spirit comes in we see only along the line of our prejudices. When we let the Holy Spirit come in, He will blow away the lines of our prejudices with His dynamic power, and we can begin to go in God's light.

A darkened heart is a terrible thing, because a darkened heart may make a person peaceful. A person says, "My heart is not bad, I am not convicted of sin; all this talk about being born again and filled with the Holy Spirit is so much absurdity." The natural heart needs the gospel of Jesus, but it does not want it, it will fight against it, and it takes the convicting Spirit of God to make men and women know they need to experience a radical work of grace in their hearts.

32
How Much Do You Love the Lord?

"If anybody comes to Me, and does not *hate* his father, and mother, ... he cannot be My disciple." That word *hate* appears to be a stumbling block to a great number of people. It is quite conceivable that many persons have such a slight regard for their fathers and mothers that it is nothing to them to separate from them; but the word *hate* shows by contrast the kind of love we ought to have for our parents, an intense love; yet, says Jesus, our love for Him is to be so intense that every other relationship is hatred in comparison if it should conflict with His claims.

Love for the Lord is not an ethereal, intellectual, dreamlike thing; it is the most intense, the most vital, the most passionate love of which the human heart is capable. The realization of such a fathomless love is rarely conscious, saving in some supreme crisis akin to martyrdom. In the generality of our days our love for God is too deeply imbedded to be conscious; it is neither joy nor peace, it is "Me" obsessed by God in the unconscious domain. Love, to be love, is deeper than I am conscious of, and is only revealed by crises. This intense personal love is the only kind of love there is, not Divine *and* human love.

33
Offend, but Do Not Cause Others to Stumble

There is a difference between "offense" and "stumbling." *Offense* means going contrary to someone's private opinion, and it is sometimes our moral duty to give offense. Did Jesus Christ know that He was offending the private opinion of the Pharisees when He allowed His disciples to pluck the ears of corn and eat them on the Sabbath day? … Certainly He did; and yet our Lord never put an occasion of stumbling in anyone's way.

Stumbling, then, is different from offense. For example, someone who does not know God as well as you do, loves you and continually does what you do because he loves you, and as you watch him, you begin to discern that he is degenerating spiritually, and to your amazement you find it is because he is doing what you are doing. Paul works this out from every standpoint in 1 Corinthians 8 and 9. "As long as I live," he says, "I will never again do those things whereby my brother is made to stumble.… I will not insist on my rights, on my liberty of conscience, but only on my right to give up my rights."

34.
Withhold Judgment

It is an easy thing to argue from precedent because it makes everything simple, but it is a risky thing to do. Give God "elbow room"; let Him come into His universe as He pleases. If we confine God in His working to religious people or to certain ways, we place ourselves on an equality with God. It is a good thing to be careful in our judgment of other men. A man may utter apparently blasphemous things against God and we say, "How appalling"; but if we look further we find that the man is in pain, he is maddened and hurt by something. The mood he is talking in is a passing one and out of his suffering will come a totally different relationship to things.

We must drop our measuring rods for God and for our fellow men. All we can know about God is that His character is what Jesus Christ has manifested; and all we know about our fellow men presents an enigma which precludes the possibility of the final judgment being with us.

35

Give God "Elbow Room"

There is a saying of Bacon's to the effect that if prosperity is the blessing of the Old Testament, adversity is the blessing of the New; and the apostle Paul says that "all who desire to live godly in Christ Jesus will suffer persecution" (2 Tm 3:12).

In every life there is one place where God must have "elbow room." We must not pass judgment on others, nor must we make a principle of judging out of our own experience. It is impossible for a man to know the views of Almighty God. Preaching from prejudice is dangerous, it makes a man dogmatic and certain that he is right. The question for each of us to ask ourselves is this: Would I recognize God if He came in a way I was not prepared for—if He came in the bustle of a marriage feast, or as a carpenter? Keep your life so constant in its contact with God that His surprising power may break out on the right hand and on the left. Leave room for Him to come in as He likes and not how you want.

36
The Christian as Intellectual Agnostic

The apostle Paul says that creation is all out of gear and twisted; it is "waiting for the manifestation of the sons of God." In the meantime, the problem remains.

Look at the world through either a microscope or a telescope and you will be dwarfed into terror by the infinitely minute or the infinitely great; both are appalling. When you touch the cosmic force, apart from the blinkers of intellect, there is a wild problem in it. Nature is wild, not tame. No man is capable of solving the riddle of the universe because the universe is mad, and the only thing that will put it right is no man's reason, but the wisdom of God which is manifested in the redemption of Jesus Christ. A Christian is an avowed agnostic intellectually; his attitude is, "I have reached the limit of my knowledge, and I humbly accept the revelation of God given by Jesus Christ."

37
Authentic Authority

Autocratic authority means to rule by right of insistence, not necessarily by right of personal integrity. Napoleon said of Jesus Christ that He had succeeded in making every human soul an appendage of His own because He had the genius of holiness. Others exercised authority by coercive means. Jesus Christ never did; His authority was worthy. He proved Himself worthy not only in the domain of God, which we do not know, but in the domain of man, which we do know; He is worthy there, consequently He prevails to open the book (see Rv 5). Authority, to be lasting, must be of the same order as that of Jesus Christ; not the authority of autocracy or coercion, but the authority of worth, to which all that is worthy in a man bows down. It is only the unworthy in a man that does not bow down to worthy authority.

38
Faith and Experience

There is a great difference between Christian experience and Christian faith. The danger of experience is that our faith is made to rest in it, instead of seeing that our experience is simply a doorway to God Himself. The reason many of us refuse to think and discover the basis of true religion is because evangelical Christianity has been stated in such a flimsy way. We get at Truth through life and personality, not by logic or scientific statements. "Therefore, I have uttered what I did not understand, things too wonderful for me, which I did not know." In refusing to stand by what was not true, Job uttered bigger things than he understood at the time. That is the way God uses men when they are rightly related to Him; He conveys His real presence as a sacrament through their commonplace lives.

39
Hearing the Voice of God

Very few of us hear the call of God because we are not in the place to answer; the call does not communicate because we have not the nature of the One who is calling. In the case of Isaiah, his soul was so attuned because of the tremendous crisis he had passed through, that the call of God was recorded to his amazed soul. God did not lay a strong compulsion on Isaiah. Isaiah was in the presence of God and he overheard, as it were, the soliloquy of God: "Whom shall I send, and who will go for Us?" and in conscious freedom he replied, "Here am I! Send me."

The call of God is not the echo of my nature, but expresses God's nature. The call of God does not consider my affinities or personality. It is a call that I cannot hear as long as I consider my personality or temperament. But as soon as I am brought into the condition Isaiah was in, I am in a relationship to God whereby I can hear His call.

40

A Perfect Place to Begin

A child is a perfect human being, so is an adult; what is the difference? The one is not yet grown, the other is full grown. When we are sanctified, we are perfectly adjusted to God but we have done nothing yet, we are simply perfectly fit to begin. The whole life is right, undeserving of censure in the sight of God; now we can begin to attain in our bodily life, to prove that we are perfectly adjusted.

We are in the quarry now and God is hewing us out. God's Spirit gathers and marks the stones, then they have to be blasted out of their holdings by the dynamite of the Holy Spirit to be chiseled and shaped, and then lifted into the heavenly places. God grant that many may go through the quarrying and the chiseling and the placing. Think of the scrutiny of Jesus Christ that each one of us has to face! Think of His eyes fastening on us and pointing us out before God as He says, "Father, that is My work; that is the meaning of Gethsemane, that is the meaning of Calvary. I did all that man's work in him, all that woman's work in her; now You can use them."

41
Servant of the Master

Yet it was well, and Thou hast said in season
As is the Master shall the servant be:
Let me not subtly slide into treason,
Seeking an honor which they gave not thee:

Never at even, pillowed on a pleasure,
Sleep with the wings of aspiration furled,
Hide the last mite of the forbidden treasure,
Keep for my joys a world within the world.

He as He wills shall solder and shall sunder,
Slay in a day and quicken in an hour,
Tune Him a chorus from the Sons of Thunder,
Forge and transform my passion into power.

42

We Are Not Our Own

We are apt to think of ourselves as our own, of the work as our work. A great point in spiritual nobility has been reached when we can really say, "I am not my own." It is only the noble nature that can be mastered—an unpalatable truth if we are spiritually stiff-necked and stubborn, refusing to be mastered. The Son of God is the Highest of all, yet the characteristic of His life was obedience. We have to learn that God is not meant for us, it is we who are meant for God. Jesus Christ does satisfy the last, aching abyss of the human heart, but that must never lead to thinking of God the Father, God the Son, and God the Holy Spirit as an almighty arrangement for satisfying us. "Do you not know that … you are not your own?" (1 Cor 6:19). It is this realization that is wrought in us by the Holy Spirit.

43
Spiritual Burnout

How sad it is to see men and women who did begin to work for God, and whose work God honored, slowly fall off. Why? They have caught the disease of death among the people they have been dealing with. [Those] in the medical profession, particularly doctors who deal with the insane, have continually to be changed, continually shifted. Why? Because they take the diseases and troubles they live among, and you will find that God the Holy Spirit has an amazing power of shifting His workers. Some wonder why God keeps shifting them, why He shifts their circumstances; the reason is not only to keep them in touch with the great sphere of work, but to keep their souls alive.

Do remember, then, that it is necessary for the worker to be healthy, and beware of this mistake: that by working for God among people, you develop your own Christian life; you do not unless your Christian life is there first.

44
Jesus Warms the Frozen Soul

Are you in constant contact with frozen natures in your own family, in your business, in your friendships? You have talked with them, prayed with them, you have done everything you know how, but there is not the slightest sign of conviction of sin, no trouble of conscience or heart. They are not out-and-out sinners, but you know that they are in-and-in sinners; you know they are wrong and twisted and have things that are not clean, but you cannot make them realize it; they always get away, frozen and untouched. Then bring your own soul face to face with Jesus Christ: "Lord, do I believe that You can thaw that man's nature, that woman's nature, until the Holy Spirit has a chance of saving him or her?" That is the first difficulty to be overcome—what state of faith in Jesus Christ have I? Then next ask yourself, do I believe that the Lord Jesus Christ can take that selfish, sensual, twisted, self-satisfied nature that is all wrong and out of order—do I believe that He can make it perfect in the sight of God? Oh, do let us get back to this tremendous confidence in the Lord Jesus Christ's power! Back to reliance on the Holy Spirit, and to remembering that Jesus came to seek the lost.

45
"Fishing" for Souls

Jesus Christ told the disciples He would make them fishers of men, catchers of human souls. Unless we have this divine passion for souls burning in us because of our personal love for Jesus Christ, we will quit the work before we are much older. It is an easy business to be a [spiritual] fisherman when revival signs are abroad; but God is wanting those who [will persevere] through long nights, through difficult days of spiritual toil. Oh the skill, the patience, the gentleness, and the endurance that are needed for this passion for souls; a sense that people are perishing doesn't do it; only one thing will do it—a blazing, passionate devotion to the Lord Jesus Christ, an all-consuming passion. Then there is no night so long, no work so hard, and no crowd so difficult, but that love will outlast it all.

46

The Christian Life Is a Holy Life

When we ask people to give themselves to Jesus Christ, do we know what we are telling them to do? We are telling them to kill forever their right to themselves, we are telling them that they have to be holy, chaste to the last recess of their bodily lives. May we remember the next time we go forth to speak for God that our bodies are the temples of the Holy Spirit. When we realize this and bind ourselves to those who realize the same truth, God will begin to do His marvels in saving individuals to Himself. So many of us are being caught up by the benedictions that fall on the crowd outside. The crowd outside will magnify the power of God, but none of those who are not right with God dare join us. A Holy Spirit movement always brings impostors, parasites, by the legion. The only safeguard for the Christian worker is "holiness to the Lord" (Ex 28:36). If we are living rightly with God, living holy lives in secret and in public, God puts a wall of fire round about us. Beware of calling anything holiness that is only winsome and sweet to the world. God grant we may never lose the touch of God that produces the holy dread.

47
The Attraction of a Holy Life

When the holiness of God is manifested in human lives and in preaching (and the two go together), these two things happen: a great number dare not join themselves, and multitudes are added to the Lord. Never think that the blessing and benediction of God on the outside crowd is all. It is a mere fringe. Men and women are blessed, their bodies are healed, devils are turned out; but the point is that multitudes of those who believe are added to the Lord. God grant that we may stand steadfastly true to Him and live this holy life. As we go forth tonight, let us remember Jesus Christ's commission, "All authority has been given to Me in heaven and on earth. Go therefore and make disciples of all nations" (Mt 28:18-19). As we examine our hearts before God, let us renew our covenant with Him.

48
New Life out of Chaos

When a man sees the light of God for the first time, it produces conviction of sin, and he cries out, "Depart from me; for I am a sinful man, O Lord." When the Holy Spirit comes into a man, "his beauty is consumed away"; the perfectly ordered completeness of his whole nature is broken up. Then the Holy Spirit, brooding over the resulting chaos, brings a word of God, and as that word is received and obeyed, a new life is formed.

"And the spirit of God was hovering over the face of the waters. Then God said, 'Let there be light'; and there was light" (Gn 1:3). God's word creates by its own power. God speaks and His word performs what He sends it to accomplish (see Is 55:11).

49
Fleshly Temple

Jesus says we should let the very corpuscles of our blood, every nerve and cell of our flesh, exhibit the new life that has been created in us.

"Do you not know that your body is the temple of the Holy Spirit who is in you?" This bodily temple of the Holy Spirit is a fleshly temple, not a spiritual one. The whole meaning of being born again and becoming identified with the death of Christ is that His life might be manifested in our mortal flesh. When we are born from above, the life of the Son of God is born in us, and the perfection of that life enables us not only to know what the will of God is, but to carry out His will in our natural human life.

50
Red-Handed Rebellion

Sin is not part of human nature as God designed it. The Bible looks on sin, not as a disease, but as red-handed rebellion against the Creator. The essence of sin is: "I won't allow anybody to boss me except myself," and it may manifest itself in a morally good person as well as in a morally bad one. Sin is not about morality or immorality; it has to do with my claim to my right to myself, a deliberate and emphatic independence of God, though I cover it with a veneer of Christian phraseology. If I allow this spirit to get back into me, I become the embodiment of heaven and hell in conflict.

51
"I Could Never Do That!"

Never disassociate yourself from anything any human being has ever done, saying, "I don't know how anyone could do that. I could never do such a thing." That is the delusion of a moral lunatic. God will give you such a knowledge of yourself that you will know, in humility before Him, how the vilest crime could be committed. You won't say, "But I could never do that"; you could. Any human being is capable of doing what other human beings have done. When you see a criminal and feel instantly, "How horrible and vile that person is," it is a sure sign that the Lord is not in you. When He is in you, you feel not only the vileness of the crime, but say of yourself, "But for God, I am that, and much worse." This is no pious phrase to be dashed off glibly; it is the awe-ful reality of our sinful nature.

52
Faith in Adversity

There is nothing akin to faith in the natural world. Defiant pluck and courage are not faith. It is the *trial* of faith that is "much more precious than gold," and the trial of faith is never without the essentials of temptation. It is doubtful whether any child of God ever gets through the trial of his faith without at some stage being horror-struck: what God does comes as a stinging blow, and he feels the suffering is not deserved. Yet, like Job, he will neither listen to nor tell lies about God.

Spiritual character is only developed as Noah's was—by standing loyal to God's character, no matter what distress the trial of faith brings.

53
Saved by Judgment

The pronouncement of coming doom contains both judgment and deliverance, for when God destroys the unsaveable, He liberates the saveable. Consequently, judgment days are the great mercy of God because they separate good and evil; they set apart right from wrong.

Salvation is always a judgment inasmuch as it involves some kind of separation: "The Cross condemns men to salvation." We remain indifferent to the Cross until we realize by the conviction of the Spirit of God that there are certain things in us which are damnable. We can always know the kind of disposition we have by the sword God brings against us. We may plead and pray, but He is merciless; He saves us "so as by fire." Once we are willing to agree with God's condemnation in the Cross, God in His infinite mercy saves us by His judgment. It is not judgment inaugurating salvation, but judgment that *is* salvation—with nations and with the human race.

54
"Why Doesn't God Save Me?"

God does not do certain things without the cooperation of man. We continually ask, "Why doesn't God do the thing instead of waiting for me?" The answer is that He chooses not to do so. It is like the difference between God's order and His permissive will. His permissive will allows the Devil to do his worst and allows me to sin as I choose, until I choose to resist the Devil, quit sinning, and come to God in the right relationship through Jesus Christ. It is God's will that human beings should get into moral relationship with Him, and His covenants are for that purpose. "Why doesn't God save me?" some ask. He has saved them, but they have not entered into relationship with Him. "Why doesn't God do this and that?" they ask. He has done it. But the point is, will we step into covenant relationship with Him?

55
Give God Your Broken "Toys"

We can pour into the bosom of God the cares that give us pain and anxiety in order that He may solve for us, and before us, the difficulties we cannot solve. We injure our spiritual life when we simply dump the real union with God. Instead, we must dump ourselves down in the midst of our problems and watch God solve them for us.

"But I have no faith," you may say. Bring your problems anyway; then stay with God while He solves them, and God Himself and the solution of your problems will be forever your own.

If we could see the floor of God's immediate presence, we would find it strewn with the "toys" of God's children who have said, "This is broken. I can't play with it anymore. Please give me another present." Only one in a thousand sits down in the midst of it all and says, "I will watch my Father mend this and see how He does it." God must not be treated as a hospital for our broken toys, but as our Father.

56
Faith, Not Fate

When God says, "Follow Me," He never says to where; the itinerary must be left entirely to Him. We come in with our "but" and "supposing" and "what will happen if I do?" (see Lk 9:57-62). We have nothing to do with what will happen if we obey; we have to abandon to God's call in unconditional surrender, leaving behind all our shivering wisdom, and smilingly wash our hands of the consequences. However, this does not mean that a life of faith is a life of fate. Fate is stoical resignation to an unknown force. Faith is commitment to One whose character we know because it has been revealed to us in Jesus Christ. And as we live in contact with our heavenly Father, His order comes to us in the haphazard, and we recognize that every detail of our lives is engineered by Him.

57
Recycling God's Gifts

Worship is the most personally sacred act that God demands of His faithful ones. Whenever God has given us a blessing, we must take time to meditate on the blessing and offer it back to God in a deliberate ecstasy of worship. He never allows us to hug a spiritual blessing to ourselves; it has to be given back to Him so that He may make it a blessing to others. If we hoard our blessings, they will turn to spiritual dry rot. If God has blessed you, erect an altar and give the blessing back to God as a love-gift.

Abraham pitched his tent between Bethel and Ai. Bethel is the symbol of communion with God; Ai is the symbol of the world. The measure of the worth of our public activity for God is the private, profound communion we have with Him.

58

Surprised by Discipline

We must never lose sight of the necessity for discipline in the life of faith; only by means of this discipline are we taught the difference between the natural interpretation of what we call good and what God means by good. We have to be brought to the place of hearty agreement with God as to what He means by good, and we only reach it by the trial of our faith, never by a stoical effort that says, "Well, I must make up my mind that this is God's will, and that it is best."

At times it appears as if God has not only forsaken His word, but has deliberately deceived us. We asked Him for a particular thing, or related to Him in a certain way, and expected that it would mean the fullness of blessing. What we got was just the opposite—upset, trouble, and difficulty all around—and we are staggered, until we learn that by this very discipline God is bringing us to the place of entire abandonment to Himself.

59
A Lesson in Obedience

Then Sarai said to Abram, "You are responsible for the wrong I am suffering. I put my servant in your arms, and now that she knows she is pregnant, she despises me. May the Lord judge between you and me." "Your servant is in your hands," Abram said. "Do with her whatever you think best." Then Sarai mistreated Hagar; so she fled from her (Gen. 16:5-6).

Sarah's passionate outbreak and her subsequent harsh treatment of her maid Hagar are examples of the way we wound our own souls and injure other lives when we try to take God's providence into our own hands.

Hagar represents the natural life when it gets out of place and takes precedence over the spiritual life. Our natural life must be in subordination and under the absolute control of the spiritual. The natural must be turned into the spiritual by obedience, whatever sword has to go through its heart.

60
God's Plan Is Best

Human free will is God's sovereign work. We have power not to do God's will, and we have that power by the sovereign will of God; but we can never thwart God's will. God allows ample room for man and the Devil to do their worst. He allows the combination of other wills to work out to the last lap of exhaustion so that that way need never be tried again, and men will have to confess, reluctantly or willingly, that God's purpose was right after all. And this holds true in the individual lives of God's children. We are at liberty to try every independent plan of our own, but we shall find in the end—whether too late or not is another matter—that what God said we had better do at the beginning was the right thing, if only we had listened to Him.

61
Come to the Feast

Times of feasting reveal a man's master like nothing else in human life, and it was in those times that our Lord revealed Himself to be Master. In like manner, our treatment of Jesus Christ is revealed in the way we eat and drink. If we are gluttons, we put Him to shame; if we are ascetics, we refuse to fellowship with Him. But when we become humble saints, we honor Him and celebrate with Him in the ordinary ways of daily life.

The Lord's Supper is a symbol of what we should be doing all the time. It is not a memorial of One who has gone, but of One who is always here. "This do in remembrance of Me" says that we should be in such fellowship with Him that we show His death until He manifests Himself again. He chose the common bread and wine to show us that the evidence of the discipline of fellowship takes place in the common elements and events of life.

62

The Riches of Poverty

We say, "It seems out of all proportion that God should choose me—I am of no value"; the reason He chooses us is that we are not of any value. It is folly to think that because a man has natural ability, he must make a good Christian. People with the best natural equipment may make the worst disciples because they will "boss" themselves. It is not a question of our equipment, but of our poverty; not what we bring with us, but what He puts in us; not our natural virtues, our strength of character, our knowledge, our experience; all that is of no avail in this matter; the only thing that is of avail is that we are taken up into the big compelling of God and made His comrade (1 Cor 1:26-28). His comradeship is made out of men who know their poverty.

63
God's Mysterious Presence

We come to God not with faith in His goodness but with a conception of our own, and we look for God to come to us in that way. God cannot come to us in our way; He can only come in His own way—in ways man would never dream of looking for Him. In the Incarnation the eternal God was so majestically small that the world never saw Him. And this is still true today. We cry out, "Oh God, I wish you would come to me," when He is there all the time. Then suddenly we see Him and say, "Surely the Lord is in this place, and I knew it not." We expect desolation and anguish; instead there is laughter and hilarity when we see God.

64
The Strength of Submission

We are apt to deify willfulness and independence and call them strength. What we call strength of will, however, God looks upon as contemptible weakness. The Being with the greatest will was our Lord Jesus Christ, and yet He never exercised His will, at least not as we think of will. His life was one of meekness and submission (see Jn 5:19, 30). There was nothing independent or willful or self-assertive about our Lord, and He says, "Learn of Me, for I am meek and lowly in heart." Jesus Christ cannot give us a meek and quiet spirit; we have to take this yoke—His yoke—upon ourselves. That is, we deliberately have to discipline ourselves.

The Sermon on the Mount teaches the destruction of individuality and the exaltation of personality. When the personal life is merged with God, it will manifest the characteristics of God.

65
How to Find God's Will

There is only one way to find out what the will of God is, and that is by not trying to find out. If you are born again in the Spirit of God, you are in the will of God, and your ordinary, common-sense decisions are God's will for you unless He gives an inner check. When He does, call a halt immediately and wait on Him. Be renewed in the spirit of your mind that you may make out His will in practical living. God's will in my common-sense life is not for me to *accept* conditions and say, "Oh well, it is the will of God," but to *apprehend* them. Doing the will of God is an active thing in my common-sense life.

66
The Hiddenness of True Piety

Though God wants our immediate and constant attention, He is never in a hurry. Abraham had to travel many long hours to the place of sacrifice; this was a journey of isolated reflection for God's servant. And it is evident that Isaac never guessed what was going on between his father and God during that journey—nor did Abraham by word or deed reveal it.

Never reveal to anyone the profound depths of your isolation; when the life of faith is dealing profoundly with God, conceal it. It was this about our Lord that staggered the Pharisees, who wanted everyone to "see" the evidences of their faith. (Piety always pretends to be going through what it is not.) When He might easily have been absorbed in the tremendous moment which He knew was at hand, He revealed no concern for Himself, only for His disciples: "Let not your heart be troubled."

67
A Sacramental Sacrifice

Abraham did not receive an overt command to sacrifice the ram; he recognized in the ram a divine suggestion. When people are intimate with one another, they can communicate by the power of suggestion; and when we come into true fellowship with God, we recognize His suggestions.

Abraham offered the ram as a substitute for his son, and the entire system of sacrifice and substitution is prefigured in this sacrifice of the ram. The spiritual sacrifice of Isaac and the physical sacrifice of the ram are made one; the natural and the spiritual are blended. I, a guilty sinner, can never get right with God; it is impossible. I can only be brought into union with God by *identification with* the One who died in my place. No sinner can get right with God on any other ground than the ground that Christ died in his stead.

68
Beware of Sweet-Sounding Sinners

One significant thing to notice is that [Isaac's future wife] Rebekah came alone and unveiled and conversed freely with a stranger (see Gn 24). Eliezer's self-forgetfulness and Rebekah's own intuition made her know that she was safe with him. There are those who talk like angels, yet they smudge the soul; there are others who may not talk sweetly yet they exhilarate the soul. Guard your intuition as the gift of God. You cannot judge virtue by its opposite; you can only judge virtue by intuition. Woe be to anyone who ignores the intuitive warning that says: Now draw back. For God's sake and your own, draw back; it matters not who the person is.

69
The Source of True Greatness

It is not what a man achieves, but what he believes and strives for that makes him noble and great. Hebrews 11 expresses this in its elevation of the life of faith above the life of human perfection. The first thing faith in God does is to remove all thought of perfection. Some lives may seem humanly perfect and yet not be relevant to God and His purpose. The effect such lives leave is not of a reach that exceeds its grasp, but of a completed little circle of its own. It takes a man completely severed from God to be perfect in that way. There is a difference between a perfect human life lived on earth and a personal life with God lived on earth; the former grasps that for which it reaches, the latter is grasped by that which it never can reach. The former chains us to earth by its very completeness; the latter causes us to fling ourselves unperplexed on God.

70

God Meets Our Deepest Needs

It is in the dark night of the soul that the realization of God's presence breaks upon us. We never see God as long as, like Esau, we are perfectly satisfied with what we are. When we are certain that "in me dwelleth no good thing," we begin to experience the miracle of seeing and hearing, not according to our senses, but according to the way the Holy Spirit interprets the Word of God to us. When the revelation of God's presence does come, it comes to those who are where Jacob was—in downright need and depression, with no vestige of human sufficiency—knowing there is no help anywhere saving in God. There, in "that place," where it is not within the bounds of human imagination to believe that God could be, He comes to us. And there is always an amazed surprise when we find what God brings with Him when He comes, for He brings everything!

71
Work & Worship & Pray

We get the idea that the best thing to do is to hurry over our work in order to get a time alone with God, and when we do get it along that line it is mildewed, not fresh and vigorous, and we feel dissatisfied instead of refreshed. Then sometimes in the midst of our work there suddenly springs up a wonderful well of inner contemplation, which is so full of recreation that we thank God for it, and we don't know how it came.

There are not three stages in spiritual life—worship, waiting, and work. Some of us go in jumps like spiritual frogs, we jump from worship to waiting, and from waiting to work. God's idea is that the three should go together. They were always together in the life of our Lord.

72
Fruit of Obedience

My personal life may be crowded with small, petty incidents altogether unnoticeable and mean, but if I obey Jesus Christ in the haphazard circumstances, they become pinholes through which I see the face of God. When I stand face to face with God, I shall discover that through my obedience thousands were blessed.

73
God's Holy Love

God and love are synonymous. Love is not an attribute of God, it *is* God. Whatever God is, love is. If your conception of love does not agree with justice and judgment, purity and holiness, then your idea of love is wrong.

The springs of love are in God, that means they cannot be found anywhere else. It is absurd for us to try and find the love of God in our hearts naturally; it is not there any more than the life of Jesus Christ is there. Love and life are in God and in Jesus Christ and in the Holy Spirit whom God gives us, not because we merit Him, but according to His own particular graciousness.

74
God's Mysterious Will

"Why does God bring thunderclouds and disasters when we want green pastures and still waters?" Bit by bit we find, behind the clouds, the Father's feet; behind the lightning, an abiding day that has no night; behind the thunder, "a still small voice" that comforts with a comfort that is unspeakable.

God's permissive will is the means whereby His sons and daughters are to be manifested. We are not to be like jellyfish saying, "It's the Lord's will." We have not to put up a fight before God ... but to wrestle before God with things.

75

Growing Souls

"Great men are not always wise, nor do the aged always understand justice" (Job 32:9).

Our physical life is meant to express all that is in our spirit. The soul struggles in travail of birth until the zone of expression in the body is reached. Paul is stating just this idea when he says, "My little children, for whom I labor in birth again until Christ is formed in you" (Gal 4:19). To begin with we have not our own bodies, but probably a body which is very much like that of one of our grandmothers or grandfathers, but every few years the physical form alters, and it alters into the shape of the ruling spirit. We may find a beautifully molded face begin to take on a remarkably ugly moral expression as it grows older, or we may find an ugly face begin to take on a remarkably beautiful moral expression. Sooner or later, through the turmoil in the soul, the physical life must express the ruling spirit. If that spirit is the spirit of the human, one shall grow further and further away from the image of God; but if one has the Spirit of God within, one shall grow more and more "into the same image from glory to glory" (2 Cor 3:18).

76
God Creates Warriors

The love of God in Christ Jesus is such that He can take the most unfit man—unfit to survive, unfit to fight, unfit to face moral issues—and make him not only fit to survive and to fight, but fit to face the biggest moral issues and the strongest power of Satan, and come off more than conqueror.

The Devil is a bully, but when we stand in the armor of God, he cannot harm us; if we tackle him in our own strength we are soon done for; but if we stand with the strength and courage of God, he cannot gain one inch of way at all.

77
More Righteousness Than the Pharisees?

"Except your righteousness shall exceed"—not be different from but "*exceed,*" that is, we have to be all they are and infinitely more! We have to be right in our external behavior, but we have to be as right, and "righter," in our internal behavior. We have to be right not only in our words and actions but also in our thoughts and feelings.

78
Love Never Fails

"Love never faileth!" What a wonderful phrase that is! But what a still more wonderful thing the reality of that love must be; greater than prophecy—that vast forth-telling of the mind and purpose of God; greater than the practical faith that can remove mountains; greater than philanthropic self-sacrifice; greater than the extraordinary gifts of emotions and ecstasies and all eloquence; and it is this love that is shed abroad in our hearts by the Holy Ghost which is given unto us.

79
The Gift of Solitude

"And Jesus being full of the Holy Ghost returned from Jordan, and was led by the Spirit into the wilderness, being forty days tempted of the Devil. And in those days he did nothing; and when they were ended, he afterward hungered" (Mk 1:12-13).

There was nothing to mark our Lord from ordinary men except that He was insulated within. He did not choose the solitary places; He was driven by the Spirit of God into the wilderness. It is not good to be alone; evil will make a person want to be alone. Jesus Christ does not make religious hermits; He makes men and women fit for the world as it is. (See Jn 17:15.) We say, "I do wish Jesus did not expect so much of me." He expects nothing less than absolute oneness with Himself as He is one with His Father. God does not expect us to work for Him, but to work with Him.

Every man carries his kingdom within, and no one knows what is taking place in another's kingdom. "No one understands me!" Of course they don't; each of us is a mystery. There is only One who understands us, and that is God. We must hand ourselves over to Him.

80
A Word to Husbands and Wives

Paul's counsel in dealing with marriage has been misrepresented—"Wives, submit to your own husbands," because we have taken the word "submit" to mean the obedience due from a slave to his master. It is not the obedience of love. In the New Testament the word "obey" is used to express the relationship of equals. "… though He was a Son, yet He learned obedience by the things which He suffered."

"For the husband is head of the wife, as also Christ is head of the church." If Christ is the Head of the husband, he is easily the head of the wife, not by effort, but because of the nature of the essentially feminine. But if Jesus Christ is not the Head of the husband, the husband is not the head of the wife. Our Lord always touches the most sacred human relationships, and He says—You must be right with Me first before those relationships can be right; and if they hinder your getting right with Me, then you must hate them (see Lk 14:26).

81

A Living Sacrifice

There is a difference between being saved and being a disciple. Some of us are saved, "yet so as through fire." We are grateful to God for saving us from sin, but we are of no use to Him insofar as our actual life is concerned. We are not spiritual disciples. Our Lord's last command was not, "Go and save men," but, "Go, … and make disciples." We cannot make disciples of others unless we are disciples ourselves.

When a man comes to Jesus it is not sin that is in the way, but self-realization, pride, his claim to himself. "I must realize myself, I must be educated and trained, I must do those things that will help me to develop myself." Self-realization is anti-Christian. All this is vigorous paganism, it is not Christianity. Jesus Christ's purpose is to make man exactly like Himself, and the characteristic of the Son of God is not self-realization but self-expenditure. Spiritual selfishness must go—am I prepared for it to go? "If any one desires to come after Me, let him deny himself," that is, "let him give up his right to himself to Me."

82

The Cleansing Power of Christ's Life in Us

"But if we walk in the light as He is in the light, we have fellowship with one another, and the blood of Jesus Christ His Son cleanses us from all sin" (1 Jn 1:7).

When we speak of the blood of Jesus Christ cleansing us from all sin, we do not mean the physical blood shed on Calvary, but the whole life of the Son of God which was poured out to redeem the world. All the perfections of the essential nature of God were in that blood, and all the holiest attainments of mankind as well. It was the life of the perfection of deity that was poured out on Calvary, "... the church of God which He purchased with His own blood" (Acts 20:28). We are apt to look upon the blood of Jesus Christ as a magic-working power instead of its being the very life of the Son of God poured forth for men. The whole meaning of our being identified with the death of Jesus is that His blood may flow through our mortal bodies. Identification with the death of Jesus Christ means identification with Him to the death of everything that never was in Him, and it is the blood of Christ, in the sense of the whole personal life of the Son of God, that comes into us and "cleanses us from all sin."

83
Patient Evangelism

Our Lord was never impatient. He simply planted seed thoughts in the disciples' minds and surrounded them with the atmosphere of His own life. We get impatient and take men by the scruff of the neck and say: "You must believe this and that." You cannot make a man see moral truth by persuading his intellect. "When He, the Spirit of truth is come, He shall guide you into all truth."

84
Growing in the Dark Times

"Consider the lilies of the field, how they grow" (Mt 6:28). A lily is not always in the sunshine; for the greater part of the year it is hidden in the earth. "How they grow"—in the dark, only for a short time are they radiantly beautiful and sweet.... We can never be lilies in the garden unless we have spent time as bulbs in the dark, totally ignored. That is how to grow.

85

Work Out Your Salvation

"Add to your faith virtue..." (2 Pt 1:5).

"Add" means there is something we have to do. We are in danger of forgetting that we cannot do what God does, and that God will not do what we can do. We cannot save ourselves nor sanctify ourselves, God does that; and God will not give us good habits, He will not give us character, He will not make us walk aright. We have to do all that ourselves, we have to work out the salvation God has worked in.

86
We Must Become As Christians

If you are a saint, says Paul, manifest it by having the mind that was in Christ who said, "I am among you as the One who serves."

One of the essential elements of deity is the humility expressed in a baby and in Jesus Christ. "And Jesus called a little child to Him, and set him in the midst of them, and said, 'Assuredly I say to you, unless you are converted and become as little children, you will by no means enter the kingdom of heaven.'" To interpret these words to mean that we are ideally to be servants of all would end in mock humility. We cannot form the mind of Christ if we do not have His Spirit, nor can we interpret His teaching apart from His Spirit.

87
The Greatest Miracle

The task that confronted Jesus Christ was that He had to bring man, who is a sinner, back to God, forgive him his sin, and make him as holy as He is Himself; and He did it single-handed. The revelation is that Jesus Christ, the last Adam, was made to be sin, the thing that severed man from God, and that He put away sin by the sacrifice of Himself—"that we might become the righteousness of God in Him" (2 Cor 5:21). He lifted the human race back not to where it was in the first Adam, but He lifted it back to where it never was, namely, to where He is Himself. "And it has not yet been revealed what we shall be, but we know that when He is revealed we shall be like Him, for we shall see Him as He is" (1 Jn 3:2).

88
Cleansed by God's Grace

The essence of sin is my claim to my right to myself. It goes deeper down than all the sins that ever were committed. Sin can't be forgiven because it is not an act; you can only be forgiven for the sins you commit, not for a heredity. "If we confess our sins, He is faithful and just to forgive us our sins" (1 Jn 1:9); sin must be cleansed by the miracle of God's grace. It does not awaken antipathy in a man when you tell him God will forgive him his sins because of what Jesus did on the Cross, but it does awaken antipathy when you tell him he has to give up his right to himself. Nothing is so much resented as the idea that I am not to be my own master. "If anyone desires to come after Me," said Jesus, "let him deny himself" (Mt 16:24), that is, deny his right to himself, not merely give up external sins—those are execrations. The point is, am I prepared deliberately to give up my right to myself to Jesus Christ? Prepared to say, "Yes, take complete control"? If I am, Jesus Christ has gained a disciple.

89
The Aroma of Holiness

There is only one kind of human nature and that is the human nature we have all got, and there is only one kind of holiness, the holiness of Jesus Christ. Give Him elbow room, and He will manifest Himself in you, and other people will recognize Him. Human beings know human beings too well to mistake where goodness comes from; when they see certain characteristics they will know they come only from the indwelling of Jesus. It is not the manifestation of noble human traits, but of a real family likeness to Jesus. It is His gentleness, His patience, His purity—never mine. The whole art of spirituality is that my human nature should retire and let the new disposition have its way. If I will walk in the light as God is in the light, then the holy nature of Jesus manifests itself in me.

90

The Wise Response to Suffering

My temperament is an inner disposition that influences my thoughts and actions to a certain extent, that is, I am either pessimistic or optimistic according to the way my blood circulates. It is an insult to take the temperamental line in dealing with a human being, "Cheer up, look on the bright side"; there are some types of suffering before which the only thing you can do is keep your mouth shut. There are times when a person needs to be handled by God, not by his fellow man, and part of the gift of human wisdom is to know how to be reverent with what he does not understand.

91
Faith and Experience

When the baptism of the Holy Spirit came upon the early disciples it made them the written epistles of what they taught, and it is to be the same with us. Our experience is the proof that our faith is right. Jesus Christ is always infinitely mightier than our faith, mightier than our experience, but our experience will be along the line of the faith we have in Him. Have we faith to bear this testimony to those who know us—that we are what we are because of our faith in Jesus? We have faith in Jesus to save us, but do we prove that He has saved us by living a new life? I say I believe that Jesus can do this and that; well, has He done it? "But by the grace of God I am what I am" (1 Cor 15:10). Are we monuments of the grace of God, or do we only experience God's supernatural power in our work for Him?

92
God's Purifying Fire

The judgments of God are a consuming fire whereby He destroys in order to deliver; the time to be alarmed in life is when all things are undisturbed. The knowledge that God is a consuming fire is the greatest comfort to the saint. It is His love at work on those characteristics that are not true to godliness. The saint who is near to God knows no burning, but the farther away from God the sinner gets, the more the fire of God burns him.

When we speak of the wrath of God, we must not picture Him as an angry sultan on the throne of heaven bringing a lash about people when they do what He does not want. There is no element of personal vindictiveness in God. It is rather that God's constitution of things is such that when a man becomes severed from God his life tumbles into turmoil and confusion, into agony and distress; it is hell at once, and he will never get out of it unless he turns to God. As soon as he turns, chaos is turned into cosmos, wrath into love, distress into peace.

93

Imitate Christ

"Leaving us an example, that you should follow His steps" (1 Pt 2:21).

For one child to imitate another child only results in a more or less clever affectation; a child imitating his parents assists the expression of inherent tendencies, naturally and simply, because he is obeying a nascent instinct. It is to this form of imitation that Peter alludes. When a saint imitates Jesus, he does it easily because he has the Spirit of Jesus in him. Pharisaic holiness, both ancient and modern, is a matter of imitation, seeking by means of prayer and religious exercises to establish, seriously and arduously, but unregeneratedly, a self-determined holiness. The only spiritually holy life is a God-determined life. "Be holy; for I am holy" (1 Pt 1:16, quoting Leviticus 11:44, et al.).

94
God Loves Us, Good or Bad

A false idea of God's honor ends in misinterpreting His ways. It is the orthodox type of Christian who, by sticking to a crude idea of God's character, presents the teaching that says, "God loves you when you are good but not when you are bad." God loves us whether we are good or bad. That is the marvel of his love. "I have not come to call the righteous, but sinners, to repentance" (Lk 5:32)—whether there are any righteous is open to question. "The righteous have no need of Me; I came for the sinful, the ungodly, the weak." If I am not sinful and ungodly and weak, I don't need Him at all.

The presentation Jesus gives of the father is that he makes no conditions when the prodigal returns, neither does he bring home to him any remembrance of the far country—the elder brother does that. It is the revelation of the unfathomable, unalterable, amazing love of God.

95

Conquerors in a Righteous Battle

Morality is not something with which we are gifted, we make morality; it is another word for character. "Unless your righteousness [i.e., your morality] exceeds the righteousness of the scribes and Pharisees," said Jesus, "you will by no means enter the kingdom of heaven" (Mt 5:20). Morality is not only correct conduct on the outside, but correct thinking within where only God can see. No matter how a man may have been tampered with by Satan, God can remake him so that in every moral battlefield he can come off more than conqueror. Thank God He does give us the fighting chance! In certain moods we are inclined to criticize God for not making the world like a foolproof machine whereby it would be impossible to go wrong. If God had made men and women like that we would have been of no worth to Him. Jesus Christ, by His almighty redemption, makes us of the stuff that can stand the strain.

96
Spiritual Anesthesia

Anesthesia means insensibility to pain, and there is such a thing as spiritual anesthesia: God can put you to sleep while the thing hurts. Some Christians do not seem to know that they are going through things, they are so wonderfully upheld by the life and power of God within; when you begin to sympathize with them, they look at you in amazement. "Why, what have I been through?" They had never realized the battle was on. The danger is to get taken up with external tribulations and trials and when we come to the end of the day to say, "Thank God, I have just got through!" Where is "the unsearchable riches of Christ" (Eph 3:8) about that? The grace of God will make us marvelously impervious to all the onslaughts of tribulation and persecution and destitution because we are seated in heavenly places in Christ Jesus and cannot be awakened to self-pity. God sends His rough weather and His smooth weather, but we pay no attention to either because we are taken up only with the one central thing—the love of God in Christ Jesus.

97
Safe in the Light

According to the New Testament, there is such a thing as obsession by unclean, malicious, wicked spirits who will damn and ruin body and soul in hell (cf. Lk 11:21-26).

A moral empty heart is the resort of these spirits when a man is off his guard. But if a man has been born again of the Spirit of God and is keeping in the light, he cannot help going right because he is backed by the tremendous power of almighty God. What does the apostle John say?—"The wicked one does not touch him" (1 Jn 5:18). What a marvelous certainty! God grant we may be so filled with the Holy Spirit that we listen to His checks along every line. No power can deceive a child of God who keeps in the light with God. I am perfectly certain that the devil likes to deceive us and limit us in our practical belief as to what Jesus Christ can do. There is no limit to what He can do— absolutely none. "All things are possible to him who believes" (Mk 9:23). Jesus says that faith in Him is omnipotent. God grant we may get hold of this truth.

98

Innocent Ignorance

There are some things of which we must be ignorant because knowledge of them comes in no other way than by disobedience to God. In the life originally designed for Adam it was not intended that he should be ignorant of evil, but that he should know evil through understanding good. Instead, he ate of the fruit of the Tree of Knowledge of Good and Evil and thereby knew evil positively and good negatively; consequently none of us knows the order God intended. The knowledge of evil that comes through the Fall has given human nature a bias of insatiable curiosity about the bad, and only when we have been introduced into the kingdom of God do we know good and evil in the way God constituted man to know them.

99
Spiritual Beauty

The presentation of true Christian experience brings us face to face with spiritual beauty, a beauty that can never be forced or imitated because it is a manifestation from within of a simple relationship to God that is being worked out all the time. There is nothing simple except a man's relation to God in Christ, and that relationship must never be allowed to be complicated. Our Lord's childhood expresses this spiritual beauty, "And the Child grew and became strong in spirit, filled with wisdom.... And Jesus increased in wisdom and stature" (Lk 2:40, 52). Jesus Christ developed in the way God intended human beings to develop, and He exhibited the kind of life we ought to live when we have been born from above.

100
"Respectable" Sinners

As long as we speak winsomely about the meek and gentle Jesus, and the beautiful ideas the Holy Spirit produces when He comes in, people are captivated, but that is not the Gospel. The Gospel does away with any other ground to stand on than that of the Atonement. Speak about the peace of heaven and the joy of the Lord and men will listen to you; but tell them that the Holy Spirit has to come in and turn out their claim to their right to themselves and instantly there is resentment—"I can do what I like with my body; I can go where I choose." The majority of people are not blackguards and criminals living in external sin; they are clean living and respectable, and it is to such that the scourge of God is the most terrible thing because it reveals that the natural virtues may be in idolatrous opposition to God.

101
Balm for the Desolate Soul

Is yours a desolated life, deserted in soul? Then in plain honesty don't blame your father or mother or anyone in your family; don't blame the fact that you had no education or that someone thwarted you when you were sixteen or that you were heartbroken when you were twenty-four or had a business disaster when you were thirty. These things may be facts, but they are not to the point. Nothing that transpires outside me can make the tiniest difference to me morally unless I choose to let it. The desolation described by Jesus was brought on by the people of God themselves and by them alone. Is God saying to you, "You have spurned and hated and murdered My messengers"? If so, it will be a painful thing for your desolated soul to say, "Blessed is He who comes in the name of the Lord"—Blessed is the one who stabs and hurts and disillusions me as to where I am.

102

The Conquering Love of Jesus

"Yet in all these things we are more than conquerors through Him who loved us" (Rom 8:37).

No matter what actual troubles in the most extreme form get hold of a man's life, not one of them can touch the central citadel, namely, his relationship to God in Christ Jesus.

This is one of the greatest assets of the spiritual aspect of Christianity, and it seems to be coming to the fore just now. Before the War* it may have been imaginary to talk about these things in the universal sense but now they are up-to-date in thousands of lives. The "wrecks" are a fact. Moral, physical, and spiritual wrecks are all around us today. The apostle Paul is not talking of imaginary sentimental things, but of desperately actual things, and he says we are "more than conquerors" in the midst of them all, superconquerors, not by our wits or ingenuity, our courage or pluck, or anything other than the fact that not one of them can separate a man from the love of God in Christ Jesus, even though he should go into the belly of hell.

*Oswald Chambers was a chaplain during World War I.

103
Unobtrusive but Real

"It is enough for a disciple that he be like his teacher" (Mt 10:25). At first sight this looks like an enormous honor—to be like his teacher is marvelous glory—is it? Look at Jesus as He was when He was here—it was anything but glory. He was easily ignorable, except to those who knew Him intimately; to the majority of men He was as a root out of dry ground (see Is 53:2). For thirty years He was obscure, then for three years He went through popularity, scandal, and hatred; He succeeded in gathering a handful of fishermen as disciples, one of whom betrayed Him, one of whom denied Him, and all of whom forsook Him; and He says, "It is enough for you to be like that." The idea of evangelical success, church prosperity, and civilized manifestation does not come into it at all. When we fulfill the conditions of spiritual life we become unobtrusively real.

104

We Are Overcomers

The saints who satisfy the heart of Jesus are the imperial people of God forever; nothing deflects them, they are superconquerors, and in the future they will be side by side with Jesus. "To him who overcomes, I will grant to sit with Me on My throne, as I also overcame and sat down with My Father on His throne" (Rv 3:21). The glorified Lord will take up His abode with the saint who puts God first in reality, not in sentiment. "We will come to him and make Our home with him" (Jn 14:23)—the triune God abiding with the saint! Jesus Christ is made heavenly bread to us now, and there is a glorious day coming—as is even now the experience of many of His people—when the nourishment of the life is the same for the saint as for his Lord. "I will come in to him and dine with him, and he with Me" (Rv 3:20).

105
Savior First, Then Teacher

Beware of placing our Lord as Teacher first instead of Savior. That tendency is prevalent today, and it is a dangerous tendency. We must know Him first as Savior before His teaching can have any meaning for us or before it can have any meaning other than that of an ideal that leads to despair. Fancy coming to men and women with defective lives and defiled hearts and wrong mainsprings, and telling them to be pure in heart! What is the use of giving us an ideal we cannot possibly attain? We are happier without it. If Jesus is a teacher only, then all He can do is to tantalize us by erecting a standard we cannot come anywhere near. But if by being born again from above we know Him first as Savior, we know that He did not come to teach us only: *He came to make us what He teaches we should be.* The Sermon on the Mount is a statement of the life we will live when the Holy Spirit is having His way with us.

106

Blessed Are the Poor in Spirit

The Sermon on the Mount produces despair in the heart of the natural man, and that is the very thing Jesus means it to do, because as soon as we reach the point of despair we are willing to come as paupers to Jesus Christ and receive from Him. "Blessed are the poor in spirit"—that is the first principle of the kingdom. As long as we have a conceited, self-righteous idea that we can do the thing if God will help us, God has to allow us to go on until we break the neck of our ignorance over some obstacle, then we will be willing to come and receive from Him. The bedrock of Jesus Christ's kingdom is poverty, not possession; not decisions for Jesus Christ, but a sense of absolute futility, "I cannot begin to do it." Then, says Jesus, "Blessed are you." That is the entrance, and it takes a long while to believe we are poor. The knowledge of our own poverty brings us to the moral frontier where Jesus Christ works.

107
Simplicity Is Essential to Godliness

The essential element in the life of a saint is simplicity, and Jesus Christ makes the motive of godliness gloriously simple: Be carefully careless about everything except your relationship to Me. The motive of a disciple is to be well pleasing to God. The true blessedness of the saint is in determinedly making and keeping God first. Herein lies the disproportion between Jesus Christ's principles and all other moral teaching: Jesus bases everything on God-realization, while other teachers base everything on self-realization.

There is a difference between devotion to principles and devotion to a person. Jesus Christ never proclaimed a cause; He proclaimed a personal devotion to Himself—"for My sake." Discipleship is based not on devotion to abstract ideals, but on devotion to a person, the Lord Jesus Christ.

108
The Salty Tang of Saintliness

"You are the salt of the earth." Some modern teachers seem to think our Lord said, "You are the sugar of the earth," meaning that gentleness and winsomeness without curativeness is the ideal of the Christian. Our Lord's illustration of a Christian is salt, and salt is the most concentrated thing known. Salt preserves wholesomeness and prevents decay. It is a disadvantage to be salt. Think of the action of salt on a wound, and you will realize this. If you get salt into a wound, it hurts, and when God's children are amongst those who are "raw" toward God, their presence hurts. The person who is wrong with God is like an open wound, and when salt gets in it causes annoyance and distress and the person is spiteful and bitter.

How are we to maintain the healthy, salty tang of saintliness? By remaining rightly related to God through Jesus Christ.

109
Giving Under Grace

There are teachers who argue that the Sermon on the Mount supersedes the Ten Commandments, and that, because "we are not under law but under grace" (Rom 6:15), it does not matter whether we honor our fathers and mothers, whether we covet, and so forth. Beware of statements like this: There is no need nowadays to observe giving the tenth either of money or of time; we are in a new dispensation and everything belongs to God. That, in practical application, is sentimental dust-throwing. The giving of the tenth is not a sign that all belongs to God, but a sign that the tenth belongs to God and the rest is ours, and we are held responsible for what we do with it. To be under grace does not mean that we can do as we like.

The secret of all spiritual understanding is to walk in the light—not the light of our convictions, or of our theories, but the light of God (1 Jn 1:7).

110

Purity and Innocence

Purity is not a question of doing things rightly, but of the doer on the inside being right. Purity is difficult to define; it is best thought of as a state of heart just like the heart of our Lord Jesus Christ. Purity is not innocence; innocence is the characteristic of a child, and although, profoundly speaking, a child is not pure, yet its innocence presents us with all that we understand by purity. Innocence in a child's life is a beautiful thing, but men and women ought not to be innocent, they ought to be tested and tried and pure. No one is born pure: purity is the outcome of conflict. The pure individual is not the one who has never been tried, but the one who knows what evil is and has overcome it.

111
Trust in Suffering

The book of Job was produced by Solomon and his school of wisdom, and in it we see worked out, according to Hebrew wisdom, how a man may suffer in the actual condition of things. The sufferings of Job were not in order to perfect him (see Jb 1:8). The explanation of Job's suffering was that God and Satan had made a battleground of his soul, and the honor of God was at stake.

The sneer of Satan was that no one loved God for His own sake but only for what God gave him. Satan was allowed to destroy all Job's blessings, and yet Job did not curse God; he clung to it that the great desire of his heart was God Himself and not His blessings. Job lost everything he possessed, including his creed; the one thing he did not lose was his hold on God, "Though He slay me, yet will I trust Him."

112

God Brings Meaning and Order in Chaos

"The sun also rises, and the sun goes down, and hastens to the place where it arose. The wind goes toward the south, and turns around to the north; the wind whirls about continually, and comes again on its circuit" (Eccl 1:5-6).

Everything that happens in nature is continually being obliterated and beginning again. What Solomon says is not merely a poetical statement. A sunset or sunrise may thrill you for half a minute, so may beautiful music or a song, but the sudden aftermath is a terrific and almost eternal sadness. Lovers always think of what one would do if the other died; it is more than drivel. Immediately you strike the elemental in war or in nature or in love, you come to the basis of ineffable sadness and tragedy. You will never find the abiding order of joy in the haphazard, and yet the meaning of Christianity is that God's order comes to a man in the haphazard.

113

Jesus Christ Is God Among Us

Jesus Christ is God-Man. God in essence cannot come anywhere near us. To be of any use to me, He must come down to the domain in which I live; and I do not live in the clouds but on the earth. The doctrine of the Incarnation is that God did come down into our domain. The wisdom of God, the Word of God, the exact expression of God, was manifest in the flesh. That is the great doctrine of the New Testament—dust and Deity made one.

Jesus Christ has the power of introducing into us His own heredity, so that dust and Deity again become one.

114

Our Helplessness, Christ's Strength

"One of the most immutable things on earth is mutability." Your life and mine is a bundle of chance. It is absurd to say it is foreordained for you to have so many buttons on your shirt and if that is not foreordained, then nothing is. If things were foreordained there would be no sense of responsibility at all. A false spirituality makes us look to God to perform a miracle instead of doing our duty. We have to see that when we do our duty in faith in God, Jesus Christ undertakes to do everything a man cannot do, but not what a man can do.

115

The Mystery of God's Providence

There is a difference between God's order and God's permissive will. We say that God will see us through if we trust Him—"I prayed for my boy, and he was spared in answer to my prayer." Does that mean that the man who was killed was not prayed for, or that prayers for him were not answered? It is wrong to say that in the one case the man was delivered by prayer but not in the other. It is a misunderstanding of what Jesus Christ reveals. Prayer alters a man on the inside, alters his mind and his attitude to things. The point of praying is not that we get things from God, but that we learn by prayer to detect the difference between God's order and God's permissive will. God's order is—no pain, no sickness, no devil, no war, no sin: His permissive will is all these things, the "soup" we are in just now. What a man needs to do is to get hold of God's order in the kingdom on the inside, and then he will begin to see how to handle the riddle of the universe on the outside.

116

Free to Freely Choose

"A time to kill, and a time to heal; a time to break down, and a time to build up" (Eccl 3:3).

Every art, every healing, and every good can be used for an opposite purpose. Every possibility I have of producing a fine character in time, I can use to produce the opposite; I have that liberty from the Creator. God will not prevent my disobeying Him; if He did, my obedience would not be worth anything. Some of us complain that God should have made the universe and human life like a foolproof machine, so simple that there would be no possibility of going wrong. If He had, we would have been like jellyfish. If there is no possibility of being damned, there is no need for salvation.

The distresses we reap in between God's decrees for us, we, together with other human beings, are personally responsible for. If we make our lives a muddle, it is to a large extent because we have not discerned the great underlying relationship to God.

117
A Broken Heart

God is infinitely patient. He says over and over again—Not that way, My child, this is the way for you, a moral relationship with Myself. "He who is often reproved, and hardens his neck, will suddenly be destroyed, and that without remedy." God will not prevent my breaking my back; if He sees I am determined to go my own way, He won't stop me. But when my neck is broken, He lifts me up and moves me where He wants, no difficulty now. "The sacrifices of God are a broken spirit." When my heart is broken, the husk of individual relationship is merged into a personal relationship, and I find that God rehabilitates everything—He puts things back into their right fittings in me.

118

The Way of Joyful Surrender

One of the dangers in modern evangelism is that it lays the emphasis on decision for Christ instead of on surrender to Jesus Christ. That to me is a grave blunder. When a man decides for Christ, he usually puts his confidence in his own honor, not in Christ at all. No man can keep himself a Christian, it is impossible; it is God who keeps a man a Christian. Many a man is kept away from Jesus Christ by honesty—"I won't be able to keep it up." If Christianity depends on decisions for Christ, it is better to keep away from it; but our Lord tells us to come to Him because we are not able to decide—a very different proposition. Jesus Christ came for the weak, for the ungodly and the sinful, and He says, "Blessed are the poor in spirit," not—"Blessed is the man who has the power to decide and keep his vow."

It is not our vows before God that tell, but our coming before God, exactly as we are in all our weakness, and being held and kept by God.

119
The Test of Temper

"Do not hasten in your spirit to be angry, for anger rests in the bosom of fools" (Eccl 7:9).

All through the Bible, emphasis is laid steadily on patience. A man's patience is tested by three things—God, himself, and other people. An apt illustration is that of a bow and arrow in the hand of an archer. God is not aiming at what we are, nor is He asking our permission. He has us in His hands for His own purpose, and He strains to the last limit; then when He lets fly, the arrow goes straight to His goal. "Acquire your soul with patience." Don't get impatient with yourself.

120

Remember Your Creator Today

"Remember now your Creator in the days of your youth" (Eccl 12:1).

We need a personal knowledge of God through all our life. The time to discover Him for ourselves is in life's earliest morning—"And that from childhood you have known the Holy Scriptures, which are able to make you wise for salvation through faith which is in Christ Jesus" (2 Tm 3:15). "And you, fathers, do not provoke your children to wrath, but bring them up in the training and admonition of the Lord" (Eph 6:4).

In the flower of your days when life is known in its rich fullness, when the natural powers are in undiluted vigor, then make place for God in personal consciousness. The prodigal remembered his father when he had spent all. He should have remembered him, gratefully, and with increasing understanding of his love and care, when his father was bestowing on him his goods. Love gives us all things richly to enjoy, and in youth and early manhood heaps rich precious bounties upon us. God must be remembered then, else we shall grievously hurt Him, and defraud ourselves.

Sources

1. *The Place of Help*, p. 18.
2. *The Place of Help*, p. 19.
3. *The Place of Help*, p. 30.
4. *The Place of Help*, p. 43.
5. *The Place of Help*, p. 50.
6. *The Place of Help*, p. 56.
7. *The Place of Help*, p. 86.
8. *The Place of Help*, p. 98.
9. *Making All Things New*, p. 19.
10. *Making All Things New*, p. 21.
11. *Making All Things New*, p. 25.
12. *Making All Things New*, p. 91.
13. *Making All Things New*, p. 106.
14. *Making All Things New*, pp. 113-14.
15. *Making All Things New*, p. 140.
16. *Making All Things New*, pp. 144-45.
17. *Bringing Sons Into Glory*, p. 195.
18. *Bringing Sons Into Glory*, p. 199.
19. *Biblical Psychology*, p. 30.
20. *Biblical Psychology*, p. 32.
21. *Biblical Psychology*, p. 40.
22. *Biblical Psychology*, p. 44.
23. *Biblical Psychology*, p. 49.
24. *Biblical Psychology*, p. 58.
25. *Biblical Psychology*, p. 59.
26. *Biblical Psychology*, p. 61.
27. *Biblical Psychology*, p. 86.
28. *Biblical Psychology*, pp. 103-4.
29. *Biblical Psychology*, p. 114.
30. *Biblical Psychology*, p. 116.
31. *Biblical Psychology*, p. 125.
32. *Biblical Psychology*, p. 150.
33. *Biblical Psychology*, p. 177.
34. *Baffled to Fight Better*, pp. 32-33.
35. *Baffled to Fight Better*, p. 34.

36. *Baffled to Fight Better*, p. 54.
37. *Baffled to Fight Better*, p. 112.
38. *Baffled to Fight Better*, p. 131.
39. *So Send I You*, pp. 13-14.
40. *So Send I You*, p. 39.
41. *So Send I You*, p. 66.
42. *So I Send You*, p. 150.
43. *So Send I You*, p. 167.
44. *So Send I You*, pp. 172-73.
45. *So Send I You*, p. 218.
46. *So Send I You*, pp. 234-35.
47. *So Send I You*, p. 235.
48. *Not Knowing Where*, p. 16.
49. *Not Knowing Where*, p. 18.
50. *Not Knowing Where*, p. 20.
51. *Not Knowing Where*, p. 25.
52. *Not Knowing Where*, pp. 31-32.
53. *Not Knowing Where*, pp. 32-33.
54. *Not Knowing Where*, p. 37.
55. *Not Knowing Where*, pp. 99-100.
56. *Not Knowing Where*, p. 45.
57. *Not Knowing Where*, p. 50.
58. *Not Knowing Where*, p. 53.
59. *Not Knowing Where*, p. 77.
60. *Not Knowing Where*, p. 82.
61. *Not Knowing Where*, p. 97.
62. *The Place of Help*, p. 186.
63. *Not Knowing Where*, p. 117.
64. *Not Knowing Where*, pp. 121-22.
65. *Not Knowing Where*, p. 126.
66. *Not Knowing Where*, p. 135.
67. *Not Knowing Where*, pp. 139-40.
68. *Not Knowing Where*, p. 153.
69. *Not Knowing Where*, p. 158.
70. *Not Knowing Where*, p. 174.
71. *Run Today's Race*, pp. 22, 24.
72. *Run Today's Race*, p. 28.
73. *Run Today's Race*, p. 34.
74. *Run Today's Race*, p. 40.
75. *Biblical Psychology*, p. 212.
76. *Run Today's Race*, p. 55.
77. *Run Today's Race*, p. 59.

78. *Run Today's Race*, p. 67.
79. *If You Will Ask*, p. 51.
80. *Shade of His Hand*, p. 126.
81. *The Place of Help*, p. 140.
82. *The Place of Help*, pp. 169-70.
83. *Run Today's Race*, p. 86.
84. *Run Today's Race*, p. 89.
85. *Run Today's Race*, p. 90.
86. *Bringing Sons Into Glory*, p. 188.
87. *Conformed to His Image*, pp. 18-19.
88. *Conformed to His Image*, p. 21.
89. *Conformed to His Image*, p. 24.
90. *Conformed to His Image*, p. 44.
91. *Conformed to His Image*, p. 53.
92. *Conformed to His Image*, pp. 66-67.
93. *Conformed to His Image*, p. 78.
94. *Conformed to His Image*, p. 111.
95. *The Servant As His Lord*, p. 129.
96. *The Servant As His Lord*, p. 136.
97. *The Servant As His Lord*, p. 143.
98. *The Servant As His Lord*, p. 167.
99. *The Servant As His Lord*, p. 171.
100. *The Servant As His Lord*, p. 176.
101. *The Servant As His Lord*, p. 178.
102. *The Servant As His Lord*, p. 198.
103. *The Servant As His Lord*, p. 204.
104. *The Servant As His Lord*, p. 219.
105. *Studies in the Sermon on the Mount*, p. 10.
106. *Studies in the Sermon on the Mount*, p. 10.
107. *Studies in the Sermon on the Mount*, pp. 13-14.

108. *Studies in the Sermon on the Mount,* p. 16.

109. *Studies in the Sermon on the Mount,* p. 18.

110. *Studies in the Sermon on the Mount,* p. 22.

111. *Shade of His Hand,* p. 14.

112. *Shade of His Hand,* p. 18.

113. *Shade of His Hand,* p. 20.

114. *Shade of His Hand,* p. 31.

115. *Shade of His Hand,* p. 32.

116. *Shade of His Hand,* p. 38.

117. *Shade of His Hand,* p. 44.

118. *Shade of His Hand,* pp. 68-69.

119. *Shade of His Hand,* p. 103.

120. *Shade of His Hand,* pp. 165-66.

Bibliography

The publisher of this book wishes to thank Discovery House Publishers (Box 3566, Grand Rapids, MI 49501) for giving us permission to compile this book from the following of Oswald Chambers' writings.

Baffled to Fight Better

Biblical Psychology

Bringing Sons Into Glory

Conformed to His Image

If You Will Ask

Making All Things New

Not Knowing Where

The Place of Help

Run Today's Race

The Servant As His Lord

Shade of His Hand

So Send I You

Studies in the Sermon on the Mount